W9-BDL-157

HOORAY FOR POLICE OFFICERS!

by Elle Parkes

BUMBA BOOKS™

LERNER PUBLICATIONS ◆ MINNEAPOLIS

Hammond Public Library
Hammond, IN

Note to Educators:

Throughout this book, you'll find critical thinking questions. These can be used to engage young readers in thinking critically about the topic and in using the text and photos to do so.

Copyright © 2017 by Lerner Publishing Group, Inc.

All rights reserved. International copyright secured. No part of this book may be reproduced, stored in a retrieval system, or transmitted in any form or by any means—electronic, mechanical, photocopying, recording, or otherwise—without the prior written permission of Lerner Publishing Group, Inc., except for the inclusion of a brief quotation in an acknowledged review.

Lerner Publications Company
A division of Lerner Publishing Group, Inc.
241 First Avenue North
Minneapolis, MN 55401 USA

For reading levels and more information, look up this title at www.lernerbooks.com.

Library of Congress Cataloging-in-Publication Data

Names: Parkes, Elle, author.
Title: Hooray for police officers! / by Elle Parkes.
Description: Minneapolis : Lerner Publications, 2016. | Series: Bumba books—Hooray for community helpers! | Audience: K to Grade 3.
Identifiers: LCCN 2016001015 (print) | LCCN 2016015222 (ebook) | ISBN 9781512414400 (lb : alk. paper) | ISBN 9781512414714 (pb : alk. paper) | ISBN 9781512414721 (eb pdf)
Subjects: LCSH: Police—Juvenile literature.
Classification: LCC HV7922 .P367 2016 (print) | LCC HV7922 (ebook) | DDC 363.2—dc23

LC record available at https://lccn.loc.gov/2016001015

Manufactured in the United States of America
1 – VP – 7/15/16

Expand learning beyond the printed book. Download free, complementary educational resources for this book from our website, www.lernerresource.com.

Table of Contents

Police Officers Protect **4**

Police Officer Tools **22**

Picture Glossary **23**

Index **24**

Read More **24**

Police Officers Protect

Police officers protect

people and places.

Police officers are also

called cops.

Police officers work in small towns.

They work in cities too.

Where else do you think police officers work?

The police make sure people follow laws.

Sometimes people do not follow laws.

Police officers may arrest those people.

Police cars have bright
lights and sirens.
Police officers turn
them on.
Other people stop
their cars.

Police cars have computers.

Computers help the police find

people and places quickly.

Dogs work with the police.

This dog finds things by their smell.

How else might dogs help the police?

People must train to be

police officers.

They learn how to help people.

They also exercise.

Why do you think police officers need exercise?

Police officers work

long days.

Sometimes their job

is unsafe.

Why do you think a police officer's job can be unsafe?

Police officers work in many places.

They protect everyone.

Police Officer Tools

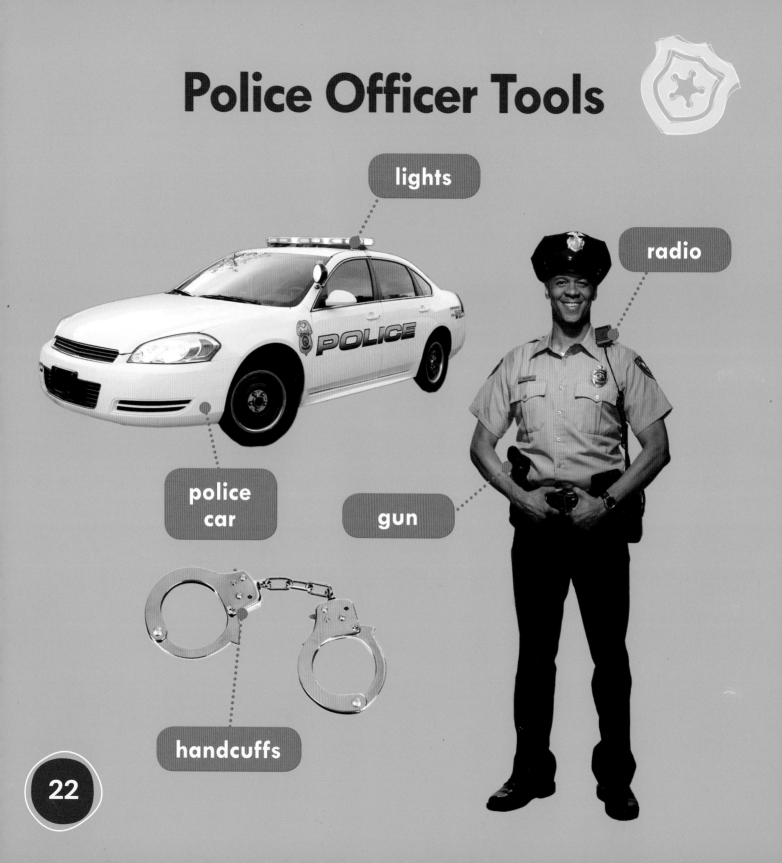

lights

radio

police car

gun

handcuffs

Picture Glossary

arrest

to stop and hold someone by the power of law

computers

electronic machines that store information

exercise

to do physical activities to stay healthy and strong

sirens

devices that make loud sounds

23

Index

arrest, 8

cities, 7

computers, 13

dogs, 14

exercise, 17

laws, 8

lights, 11

police cars, 11, 13

sirens, 11

towns, 7

Read More

Bellisario, Gina. *Let's Meet a Police Officer.* Minneapolis: Millbrook Press, 2013.

Meister, Cari. *Police Officers.* Minneapolis: Jump!, 2014.

Murray, Julie. *Police Officers.* Minneapolis: Abdo Kids, 2016.

Photo Credits

The images in this book are used with the permission of: © aijohn784/iStock.com/Thinkstock, pp. 4–5; © Supannee Hickman/Shutterstock.com, pp. 6–7, 15; © bikeriderlondon/Shutterstock.com, pp. 9, 23 (top left); © stockelements/Shutterstock.com, pp. 10–11, 23 (bottom right); © Stockbyte/Thinkstock, pp. 12, 23 (top right); © Richard Thornton/Shutterstock.com, pp. 16, 23 (bottom left); © arindambanerjee/Shutterstock.com, pp. 18–19; © Steve Debenport/iStock.com, p. 21; © Brad Sauter/Shutterstock.com, p. 22 (top left); © Siri Stafford/DigitalVision/Thinkstock, p. 22 (right); © Veronica Louro/Shutterstock.com, p. 22 (bottom left).

Front Cover: © Susan Chiang/iStock.com.

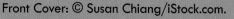
3 1161 00924 1145

Youth
2532